Intentionally Blank

Intentionally Blank

Intentionally Blank

Intentionally Blank

Intentionally Blank

Intentionally Blank

Intentionally Blank

Intentionally Blank

Intentionally Blank

Intentionally Blank

Intentionally Blank

Intentionally Blank

Intentionally Blank

Intentionally Blank

Intentionally Blank

Intentionally Blank

Intentionally Blank

Intentionally Blank

Intentionally Blank

Intentionally Blank

Intentionally Blank

Intentionally Blank

Intentionally Blank

Intentionally Blank

Intentionally Blank

Intentionally Blank

Intentionally Blank

Intentionally Blank

Intentionally Blank

Intentionally Blank

Intentionally Blank

Intentionally Blank

Intentionally Blank

Intentionally Blank

Intentionally Blank

Intentionally Blank

Intentionally Blank

Intentionally Blank

Intentionally Blank

Intentionally Blank

Intentionally Blank

Intentionally Blank

Intentionally Blank

Intentionally Blank

Intentionally Blank

Intentionally Blank

Intentionally Blank

Intentionally Blank

Intentionally Blank

Intentionally Blank

Intentionally Blank

Intentionally Blank

Intentionally Blank

Intentionally Blank

Intentionally Blank

Intentionally Blank

Intentionally Blank

Intentionally Blank

Intentionally Blank

Intentionally Blank

Intentionally Blank

Intentionally Blank

Intentionally Blank

Intentionally Blank

Intentionally Blank

Intentionally Blank